EPHESUS

132 Colour illustrations

D1313669

ⅢB BONECHI

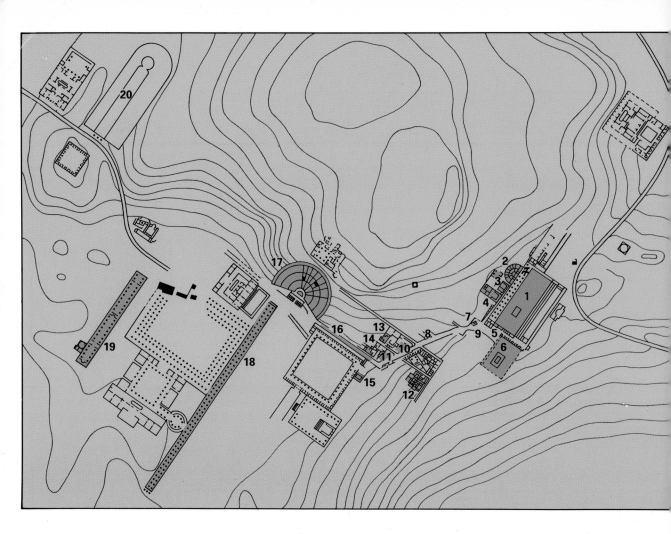

1 – AGORA
2 – ODEUM
3 – TEMPLES OF THE GODDESS ROME
    AND OF DIVINE CAESAR
4 – PRYTANEION
5 – FOUNTAIN OF POLLIONE
6 – TEMPLE OF DOMITIAN
7 – MONUMENT TO MEMMIO
8 – GATE OF HERACLES
9 – KURETES STREET
10 – FOUNTAIN OF TRAJAN

11 – TEMPLE OF HADRIAN
12 – HOUSES ON THE SLOPE
13 – BATHS OF SCHOLASTICA
14 – BROTHEL
15 – LIBRARY OF CELSIUS
16 – MARBLE STREET
17 – THE THEATRE
18 – ARCADIAN WAY
19 – CHURCH OF THE MOST
    HOLY VIRGIN
20 – STADIUM

Panorama of Selçuk.

HISTORICAL NOTES

*T*he ruins of Ephesus *take on a value and a special significance among the innumerable sites of an archaeological interest: this is* due to its inestimable artistic patrimony, its enormous heritage of history and culture, and the inexhaustible beauty and charm of its archaeological site.
The original site of Ephesus was most likely established on the Aegean coast, on the shores of that sea which today is «located» eight kilometres away from the archaeological excavations. Over the centuries, in fact, the rubble brought onto the plain of the Kükük Menderes has enlarged the alluvial plain surrounding the archaeological zone, leaving behind in actual fact the shores of the Aegean.

The foundation of Ephesus took place between the 16th and 11th centuries B.C., and this assertion is confirmed in part by subsequent archaeological findings. Certainly its founders were of Greek ancestry. In the meantime, the Ionic colonization in Asia Minor progressed rapidly, and very soon the new Ionic cities united in the Ionic Confederacy. The first events of the city were not fortunate ones: Androcles, the mythical founder, fell in battle against the Karians. Subsequently (7th century B.C.), Ephesus was the prey of the hoards of Cimmerians who brought about its total destruction, not even sparing its most lofty symbol: the Artemision.
Notwithstanding the beginnings which were any-

3

ΣΟΦΙΑ
ΚΕΛΣΟΥ

The Celsus Library, detail.   The Theatre.

thing but fortunate, the new ruling class knew how to impart a positive course to the events which culminated – under the reign of Croesus, King of the Lydians – in the construction of the new Temple of Artemis and in the virtual rebuilding of the urban city fabric (6th century B.C.). Shortly before the middle of the century, Croesus was defeated by Cyrus, King of the Persians, who very quickly subjugated other cities of Ionic original, along with Ephesus.

The presence of the Artemision and the very favorable geographical location of Ephesus played an important role in the fortunes of the town and in its historical vicissitudes. Towards the end of the 4th century B.C., the city fell firmly into the hands of Lysimachus of Thrace, who won out over the claims put forth by Demetrius Polyorcetus. Under him, the city knew a new urbanistic arrangement, with the creation of new fortifications between the high ground of Mount Coressus and Mount Pion, and with the realization of a new port to replace the ex-

isting one, subject to the phenomenon of silting-up. Likewise, Ephesus saw its own demographic consistency grow with the introduction of people coming from the destroyed cities of Colophones and Lebed Lebedos. In the same period, a Roman attempt at rebellion, inspired by Mithridates, was very short-lived.

Visits by illustrious personages such as Brutus, Cassius and Cicero gave testimony to the importance which Ephesus held in the Roman world. Risen to the actual Asiatic capital in the place of Pergamum, in the Augustan era, the city was to grow, very soon becoming an active commercial emporium, a permanent seat for the Roman governor, and one of the first five cities of the Empire. In 17 A.D. the city was razed to the ground by a disastrous earthquake. Tiberius and Hadrian, who was at Ephesus in the summer of 123 A.D., pushed for its rebuilding and further development. At the beginnings of the Christian era, Ephesus had the aspect of a magnificent Hellenic-Roman metropolis,

5

The Celsus Library.   *The Temple of Hadrian.*

considered on a level with important cities in the ancient world such as Alexandria and Antioch. The preaching of John the Apostle (buried here in the Church of the same name) and a tradition which said that the Virgin Mary chose it as her home after the Crucifixion, made of Ephesus one of the landmarks in the history of Christianity.

The decline of the city began in the second half of the third century, starting with the conquest of the Goths and the consequent devastations. In 431 Ephesus hosted the 3rd Ecumenical Council, aimed – among other things – at confuting the Nestorian heresy. In the Justinian era (6th century A.D.), the progressive turning into swamps of the various places had made it necessary to establish new seats which were traced in proximity to the Basilica of St John, erected by the same Emperor.

During the long and obscure centuries of the Middle Ages, the city – reduced to not much more than a village – was subject to the repeated forays of Arabs and pirates. During the course of the 10th and 11th centuries it was named Hagios Theologos in honour of St John. Having come into the possession of the Seljuks (1090), it subsequently belonged to the Commerians and then was aggregated (beginning of the 13th century) into the Kingdom of Nicaea. Once again in Turkish hands, starting in 1308, Ephesus was enriched by edifices bearing the typical Islamic imprint. During the 14th century the city was the Bishops' seat, frequented by Genoese and Venetian traders.

After the first years of the Ottoman domination, Ephesus fell into the most complete oblivion: abandoned and deserted, almost all its traces were lost; these were to reemerge starting in 1869, the year of the first archaeological assays undertaken by an Englishman, J. T. Wood, and then continued by the Austrians and the Turks.

THE ISA BEY MOSQUE

The monumental structure situated on the slope to the west of the Church of St John is the Isa Bey Mosque, built in 1375 by Isa Bey, one of the principal rulers of Aydınoğlu. The inscription pertaining to the contruction is on the lintel of the entrance in the west. There are entrances in the east, west and north, but the main entrance is the one in the east. These entrances lead into the courtyard. The *western façade* of the mosque, built of marble, is elaborately decorated. The high entrance is shaped like a crown and decorated with geometric motifs using black and white marble pieces to create contrast. These decorations are typical of Seljouk art. A staircase on each side leads up to the narrow podium in front of the entrance. The window frames on the western façade are beautiful examples of the art of marblework. The southern façade is plain, and the two pillars there were built to support the wide, high façade. The eastern façade faces the Church of St John and is also quite plain. In the exact center of the northern façade is the third entrance into the courtyard. The road with sidewalks extends from the fortress to this entrance which is higher than the floor of the courtyard. A few steps lead down to the *square courtyard* which is surrounded on three sides with double-tiered porticos supported by columns. The columns of the porticos which have collapsed were brought here from the ancient structures in Ephesus. There is a marble şadırvan in the middle of the courtyard and a *minaret* on top of the western entrance. The part of the minaret above the balcony is missing. On top of the eastern entrance is the *Ordeal Chamber*. The main chamber of the mosque is entered from the courtyard through a gate with three entrance ways. The *mihrap* (the niche in the direction of Mecca) is right across the entrance. During the years when the mosque was not in use, the mihrap, which is made of marble in a geometric design, was moved to another mosque in Izmir. The one seen today was made in recent years and resembles the original one. The roof of the mosque is unusual and is rarely seen elsewhere. The *dome* in the center is covered with turquoise tiles. Three granite columns support the dome and the roof. The columns and the two composite column capitals were brought here from the Harbour Baths. The third column capital has stalactites and is shaped in a manner peculiar to Turkish Seljouk art.

Basilica of St John, a stretch of the perimetral walls.

Isa Bey Mosque, general view.

The Isa Bey Mosque.

THE BASILICA OF ST JOHN

The grandiose ruins of this outstanding example of Byzantine architecture rise on the southern part of the hill which plays host to the *Castle of Selçuk*. The first Christian basilica was erected with a wooden covering in the 4th century on the burial site of John the Apostle. In fact, a consolidated Christian tradition affirmed that the evangelist had lived in Ephesus, as the Virgin Mary was said to have lived there after expulsion from Jerusalem, and that there he continued his work of evangelization, writing down his holy inspirations and being buried there according to his own wishes. In the 6th century, during the reign of Justinian (527-565), who brought Byzantine art and architecture to elevated levels of splendour, it was decided to build the imposing basilica, the ruins of which can be admired today. Between the 7th and 8th centuries, when the risk of Arab invasions hung over the city, the building was fortified by means of a powerful surrounding wall

which connected it to the Castle. In medieval times the Basilica became a much-frequented destination for Christian pilgrims, who were attracted by the sacredness of the place and by the widespread belief that the exalations coming from the apostle's tomb had beneficial therapeutic properties. In the 14th century the Basilica was destined as a place for Islamic worship: traces of the transformation into a mosque and of the foundations of the minarets can be perceived at the entrance into the narthex. In the same period, parallel with the construction of the Mosque of Isa Bey, the church lost many of the motivations which had made of it an important place of worship in previous centuries. At the end of the 14th century, a ruinous earthquake reduced to a cluster of ruins what had once been a beautiful and elegant building. Starting in the 1920's consistent excavational and restoration work has been undertaken, which has led also to the anastilosis of several

Basilica of St John, general views with the remains of the columns and portico.

Following pages, the Gate of St John and general view of the Basilica.

Basilica of St John, details of the vestibule and of one entrance (opposite) and some raised columns next to ancient jars (above).

columns discovered in the northern nave.

The original basilica structure, in the form of a cross, was copied from the model of the *Church of the Holy Apostles* in Jerusalem. On a level with the foot of the cross was the sepulchre of St John, right at the point of the original building replaced by the Justinian construction. Access to the ruins of the church is possible through a door flanked by towers, which has been opened in the fortified circle of walls. The *vestibule* is composed of a central courtyard surrounded by a columned portico (37x47 m). At the centre are gathered several amphoras from different ages.

Through a long and narrow *narthex*, originally topped by five small cupolas, was the entrance to the actual part of the Basilica in the strict sense of the word, which evidenced the classic division of the original edifice, divided by three naves, crossed transversally by the transept and surmounted by six

full cupolas. The marble columns and the brick supports which upheld the cupolas can still be seen. The fragments found give an idea of the considerable decoration which adorned the building. *The monograms of Justinian and Theodora* on the capitals facing towards the central nave constitute a valuable evidence in the dating of this building. Fragments of the cupolas, which turned up in the excavations, show traces of mosaic decorations and frescoes. The *Apostle's Sepulchre* is located opposite the apse, in the central nave, and is easily identifiable due to the fact that it protrudes. On the side of the north transept can be perceived the remains of a structure transformed into a chapel (10th century), with traces of frescoes reproducing St John, Christ and the Saints. Recent excavations have brought to light the complex structure of an octagonal *baptistery* with a central font, created in an era preceding the building of the Basilica.

THE ARTEMISION

A column and scanty fragments strewn on the ground are all that remains of the Seventh Wonder of the World. According to Strabo, the Temple of Artemis was destroyed at least seven times and rebuilt just as many times. Archaeological findings instead attest to at least four rebuildings of this temple, starting in the 7th century B.C. An Ionic dipteral temple was erected by Chersiphone and Metagene in the 6th century B.C., and its building required no less than 120 years. In 356 B.C. the temple was set on fire by Herostratus; the successive majestic structure, built entirely of marble, was begun in 334 and was finished in 250 B.C.: it aroused the admiration of even Alexander the Great, who would have liked to have taken charge – at his own expense – of the continuation of the work. Among others, Scopas and Praxiteles worked there, while the design is attributed to Chirocratus. The Hellenistic temple was built on a podium, to which one ascended by a plinth formed of thirteen steps. A double colonnade encircled the peristyle and the inside space (105x55 m). The reliefs of the columns were believed to be the work of Scopas, while Praxiteles worked at the realization of the altar. The decadence marked by the Goths (3rd c.) continued in the Christian era, when it was utilized as the «quarry» for marble and stone materials for the nearby *Basilica of St John* and for the *Church of St Sophia* at Costantinople. Very little is left of the numerous works of art which at one time used to adorn it, although interesting tokens are kept at the local *Museum* and at the *British Museum* in London.

The Artemision, the ruins and a surviving column.

The ruins which can be seen at present refer to a Roman building of the Imperial Age (1st century A.D.), probably finished off in the time of Augustus and Claudius. Archaeological findings, datable between the 7th and 6th centuries B.C., would support the hypothesis that on this site an ancient cemetry pre-existed, which has given up its tombs, a fictile sarcophagus and traces of roadway paving. The Agora, which received its final accomodation under Theodosius (4th century), was decorated with a double colonnade (*stoa*) where commercial activities were carried on. A fulcrum of mercantile activities, it was frequented by merchants coming from every corner of the Empire; it also entertained the slave market, and was the hub for civil and religious festivities.

Like all buildings of this sort, also the Agora of Ephesus presents the traces of a temple structure which rose in the centre of the spacious square (160x56 m). The foundation of this temple has definitely been identified: it supposedly had ten columns on the larger side and six on the smaller side, and dates from the 1st century B.C. It is believed that it was dedicated to the worship of Isis, even if several authorities are inclined to the hypothesis that it was the *Temple of Augustus*. The sculptural figures which once decorated the pediment were transferred to the *Fountain of Pollione*: at present they can be seen at the *Museum of Ephesus*.

A *sundial*, surrounded by statues, used to stand at the centre of the Agora: several inscriptions imprinted on the bases have given us precise information for an understanding of the social order of the ancient city. To the north of the Agora rise the cropped stones of the columns of the **Basilica** which was erected during the Augustan era. Several columns which have survived are indicative of an unmistakable doric vestige, while the coping of the capital is obviously Corinthian in its imprint.

Agora, in the northern part rise Doric columns supporting Corinthian capitals. These ruins are part of the Basilica.

Agora, ruins of the Basilica.

2 - ODEUM

This semi-circular structure, known also as the Small Theatre, is set down on the slopes of the hills to the north of the Agora. An inscription of 150 A.D. attributes its foundation to a certain Publius Vedius Antonius, who conceived it as a *Bouleuterion* or meeting place for the Senate. In reality, the original structure was provided with coverings and, with a capacity of 1,400 seated spectators, alternatively served as bouleuterion and as a small covered theatre. The architectural design partially follows this classic of analogous models of antiquity; the *auditorium* with double rows, semi-circular in form, is divided by four main wedges of stairs separated from the passageways, while the unusual structure of the proscenium clearly denotes the intention of its builders, who wanted the most suitable building for housing the meetings of the Senate, rather than theatrical performances.

Details of the Odeum. This building was meant for meetings of the town's Senate, but theatrical performances were also held there.

Below, general view of the Odeum.

3 - TEMPLES OF THE GODDESS ROME AND OF DIVINE CAESAR

In the Augustan era, the spread of Imperial-Roman cults was by then a fact in many provinces of Asia Minor. The cult of the Emperor was alive in Nicomedia and in Pergamum, together with that of the Goddess Rome. The idea for the building of a temple which could celebrate the Goddess Rome, the Roman divinity by antonomasia, together with Julius Caesar, whose divine attributes were venerated, occurred to his adoptive son, Octavius. The latter – who was to become Emperor with the name of Augustus – authorized the construction of the sanctuary on the occasion of a visit made to the Asiatic province in 29 B.C.

Its erection in the vicinity of the *Prytaneion*, constituted an aggregation point for the Romans resident in the province, and an unquestionable testimony to the important role played by Ephesus within the political and administrative organization of this important part of the Roman Empire.

The complex, composed of two separate temples, with four columns on the eastern prospect, arose on a podium surrounded on three sides by porticoed structures of pure Doric imprint. The architectural conformation of the buildings, usual in Ancient Rome, was in fact very atypical for the territories of Greece and Asia Minor. The remains of these temples have in our day been located in the immediate vicinity of the *Odeum*, in the centre of a courtyard founded by the ruins of a columned portico. The subsequent superimposing of other buildings determined the inevitable collapse: several columns supporting remains of entablature, together with ruins of perimetral walls and of the stylobate, constitute its most appreciable remains.

General view of the Odeum, Temples of the Goddess Rome and of Divine Caesar, the Prytaneion.

Temples of the Goddess Rome and of Divine Caesar, remains of columns with entablature.

4 - PRYTANEION

The considerable remains of this building were set down on the slopes of the hills, up from the Basilica. Its function in antiquity was comparable to that of our town hall: in addition to public functions, it housed important events, receptions and banquets. In the annexed *Temple of Hestia Boulaia* there burned perennially the sacred fire which the Pritanei – the priests who attended to the citizens' worship and to the sacrificial practice – had to feed.

If its construction can be dated with certainty to the 3rd century B.C. (its definitive arrangement occurred later, in the middle of the Augustan age), the

Prytaneion, details of a pedestal depicting Hermes and of an epigraph.

Prytaneion, columns supporting remains of entablature.

source which asserts the existence of a place assigned to receive the perennial fire, which symbolized the very existence of the city, at least since the Age of Lysimachus, appears to be reliable.

The most substantial surviving ruins are identifiable from two Doric columns supporting a section of entablature due to a restoration and to a fairly recent anastilosis. Other columns, stone stumps and conspicuous ruins of the city walls, reinstate the picture of a building definitely noteworthy even as to its dimensions. Its interior must have been highly ornamented: the courtyard bore a massive decoration,

while the altar on which the sacred fire burned was located at the centre of the auditorium on basaltic foundations. The composite style of the capitals upheld by the columns indicates re-coverings which date to the 3rd century A.D.

The inscriptions engraved on the architectural fragments and on the columns are very interesting, since they offer us a listing referring to the *League of the Kuretes* (these were a category of priests of the Artemision) that supplies further information on religious practices in the city. The decadence of the Prytaneion goes back to the 4th century, when it

Prytaneion, sculpture depicting a winged Nike.

Domitian Square, circular structure believed to be a Roman altar.

was used as a «quarry» of materials for the construction of the *Baths of Scholastica*. Among the numerous sculptured figurations which ornamented the edifice, the *Statue of Artemis* deserves particular mention: it is at present on display at the Museum, but it was discovered near the altar in an excellent state of preservation. On the road which links the Prytaneion to the *Monument of Memmio*, on the left, the pedestal depicting Hermes (Mercury) in the act of seizing a ram by the horns and holding the caduceus in his left hand, is worthy of note. The so-called *Domitian Square*, which opens immediately to the west of the *Agora* and below the *Monument of Memmio*, is of extreme interest because of several el-

ements located there. The circular structure which, unusually, is prominent in the centre of the square was transported there from another place in the town, around the 4th century. In all probability, it was a Roman altar made up of big blocks resting on a circular plinth. Of particular interest are the external decorations, which depict *heads of bulls supporting a garland*. In the immediate vicinity of this peculiar structure has been set up a triangular-shaped architectural element coming from the *Door of Heracles* which rises at the start of *Kuretes Street*. The sculptural figuration which is prominent there represents *Winged Nike*, the Goddess of Victory, while she holds a plaited crown in her left hand.

The ruins of this lovely and artistic architecture refer to a fountain, erected in 93 B.C. so as to enrich a monument erected between 4 and 14 A.D. dedicated to C. Sestius Pollione. He had acquired some merits with the Ephesian society of the time as he was the instigator of the *Aqueduct of Marnas*, which carried its waters to a 2nd-century fountain located south of the *Agora*, opposite the *Odeum*.

The Fountain of Pollione is located in the western vicinity of the Agora, to the east of the so-called *Domitian Square*. The elegant small arch is supported by pillars partly ornamented by reliefs and it frames the absidal semi-circular basin which houses the actual fountain. Near the wall of the apse was located the sculptural group depicting the *Myth of Polyphemus* – before its translation to the *Museum*. It seems that these sculptures originally decorated the tympanum of the *Temple of Isis*, and that they were transferred to embellish the fountain after the collapse of the edifice, located in the centre of the Agora.

Fountain of Pollione, view of the arch and the absidal basin.

Kuretes Street, view towards the fountain of Pollione.

6 - TEMPLE OF DOMITIAN

The location of the temple, to the east of the *Agora*, a little below *Domitian Square*, in a part of the city of unquestionable importance, does justice to the more than considerable opinion of the Ephesians in regard to the Roman Emperor who proclaimed himself «God and Leader». In actual fact, not much remains of this building, erected in the 1st century A.D. at the foot of Mount Bülbül, on a terrace upheld by imposing substructures (50x100 m). Several elements of the parapet, formed by a double row of columns and which preceded the remains of the temple, were located in their original place.

The devotion to Domitian, from which the Ephesians derived indiscutible privileges on account of the contruction of the temple – the first one in the city consecrated to a Roman emperor – is evident from the ruins of the colossal statue of the Emperor. The huge head (it is thought that the entire statue must have measured a good 7 metres including the base) with the forearm are kept in the *Archeological*

Museum of Izmir, while other parts can be seen at the *Museum of Ephesus*. Several remains of the altar (displayed at the local museum) reveal an execution of exceptional value. After the violent death of Domitian, the victim of an assassin, the Ephesians hastened to dedicate the temple to Domitian's father, Vespasian, so as not to have to give up the rights which they had acquired.

As the majority of Roman temples, the architectural structure of this temple was that of a small prostyle, preceded by a columned portico with a peristyle of 8 columns on the shorter side, and of 13 columns on the longer side, resting on the stylobate. Entrance to the cella was made possible by a stone block formed into eight steps. Interesting evidences of the social life and civic organization of ancient Ephesus are displayed in the so-called *Gallery of Carvings*, located in the eastern substructures of the temple, where a large quantity of epigraphs discovered during archaeological excavations have found a home.

Temple of Domitian, ruins and detail of the columned parapet.

The conspicuous remains of this structure rise in the northern part of *Domitian Square,* close to a semicircular building which dated from the late Hellenistic period (1st c. B.C.) and was erected in honour of Caius Memmio, Sylla's grandson. In 84 B.C. the latter had ordered the destruction of Ephesus because its inhabitants had flanked Mithridates, in an attempt at rebellion against Rome. The original structure of the monument, divided into a succession of triumphal arches supported by caryatids, gave evidence of the city's intention of submission. The ruins of the monument as it appears today rest on a stone base formed by four small staircases. On each façade the motif of the semicircular niches, that were connected to each other by arches decorated with blocks upholding sculptures, can still be seen. The sculptures which still decorate the monument are those of Memmio, of his father and of Sylla.

Monument to Memmio, details of the sculptures and general view.

The gate is located at the beginning of *Curetes Street* which stretches westward from the *Memmius Monument*. It is a two-storeyed edifice. In the lower storey there is a wide arched passageway, and in the upper storey there are six columns in a row. Reliefs of flying *Nikes* that are found today in Domitian Square used to be situated at the corners where the arch joins the pillars with Corinthian capitals. One of these reliefs and most of the construction fragments have not yet been found.

The two centrally-located columns at the upper level resemble the lintels of the gate. On these two columns, there are two reliefs of Heracles depicted wrapped in a Nemea lion skin. They are like the *caryatids* supporting Corinthian capitals and exhibit 2nd century craftsmanship. They were moved here in the 5th century from another location.

This street which goes up the slope between the *Library of Celsius* and the *Gate of Heracles* is certainly the most charming Ephesian artery unravelled in the centre of the ancient city. It attained its splendour at the time of restoration of the road which, towards the middle of the 4th century, had been ramshackle and made unusable by a violent and ruinous earthquake.

Its inclusion in a countryside and environment which boast elements of extreme fascination and appeal harmonizes – by means of the precious structure of marble and stone pavements – with the remains of antiquity that surround it, in a remarkable picture punctuated by columns, stumps of stone pedestals, podiums, ornamented capitals, friezes, inscriptions, statues and traces of buildings for commercial use and for use as habitations. In this vast

General view of Kuretes Street.

Kuretes Street, details of architecture.

Kuretes Street, views towards the Library of Celsius, details of sculptures and stones of columns.

profusion of antique ruins, often specially carried from other areas of the city, stand out covered columned galleries whose pavements are made precious by refined mosaics. The empty pedestals, which in great numbers face the group of columns, were once surmounted by statues: a great many of them bore several interesting engraved epigraphs. Many of the statues were transferred to the *Museum*. The name of the street refers to mythological characters who, in a later epoch, gave name to the cast of priests of the Kuretes. The latter devoted themselves in a first temple to the services which were celebrated in the *Artemision* but, subsequently, they found a place also inside the Prytaneion. Numerous inscriptions on their role can be found in different parts of the city, even if the citations of great prominence are to be found in the *Prytaneion*. It is known that their number – initially composed of six units – was later raised to nine.

Along *Kuretes Street*, in a wonderful succession of ancient ruins, sculpted pillars decorated with sculptural figurations, we can see reconstruction on a reduced scale (the original reached a height of 12 m) of one of the most remarkable Ephesian monuments. The fountain was erected between 102 and 104 A.D. and, as the attached inscription reads, was consecrated to the Emperor Trajan.

The tympanum which dominates the upper line is supported by Corinthian columns; in the central niche was once located an enormous statue of Trajan, of which only the base with the feet and the globe remain. The many sculptured figurations which once populated this fountain (*members of the Imperial Family, Dionysus, Aphrodite, Satyr*) have been carried to the Museum.

Fountain of Trajan along Kuretes Street.

Fountain of Trajan, ruins and reconstruction on reduced scale.

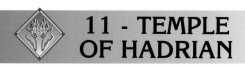
This magnificent temple has reached us in a more than acceptable state, also in consequence of the restoration works undertaken after the earthquake which destroyed it in the 4th century A.D. Its most desirable location along *Kuretes Street*, not far from the staircase which goes up to the *Baths of Scholastica*, makes it one of the most attractive and, without doubt, most sought-after destinations of the entire archaeological complex. An inscription sculpted into the architrave of the temple gives testimony to its construction around 138 A.D. by the hand of a certain P. Quintilius, who dedicated it to Emperor Hadrian. In this way there arose in the city the second place of worship dedicated to a Roman emperor, after the one previously dedicated to Domitian. Facing the monumental pronaos also arose the pedestals of four statues which formerly decorated the building. When reading the inscriptions sculpted on each of them, we learn that the carved figures depicted Roman emperors who ruled between the end of the 3rd century and the begin-

Views of Hadrian's Temple on Kuretes Street with pronaos and cella.

Kuretes Street, view from Hadrian's Temple towards the Houses on the slope.

Hadrian's Temple, details of the arch (bust of Tyche) and of the semi-circular lunette (Medusa).

ning of the 4th century, namely: Diocletian, Maximian, Constantine, Clorus and Galerius.
The temple is markedly Corinthian, and is distinguished by the precise and elegant weaving of the sculptural ornamentation which is evident even from a first superficial glance. The pronaos which precedes what is more properly known as the simple naos (*cella*) was originally closed by a vaulted covering. Today it appears with four Corinthian supports on the front. The two central columns (the more external supports are in fact pilasters) uphold the very beautiful finely-sculpted arch which is all that remains of the original triangular tympanum which once constituted the coping of the edifice. The ornamentation of the arch perpetuates the motifs of the friezes which are prominent on the entablature and culminate centrally in the *Bust of Tyche* (the Goddess who was protectress of the city). The architraved structure which stands out on the portals is embellished by a rich decoration, drawing on classical motifs. Above the main portal which gives

access to the naos is a semi-circular lunette which attracts the attention of the visitor because of its precious sculptured figurations: from an elegant interweaving of flowers and acanthus leaves, we rise to a female figure very similar to the classic effigies of *Medusa*. In the 4th century, during rebuilding works following the earthquake which brought about partial destruction, some reliefs coming from other buildings in Ephesus were added in the inside upper portion of the pronaos. Nowadays, these remarkable figurations (4th c.) can be admired in the *Ephesus Museum*, as those *in loco* are just copies. The subjects of these reliefs draw mainly on mythology: *Androcles among the Gods following the wild boar, Deities with Amazons, Dionysus with Amazons in procession, Selenius, Apollo, Androcles, Heracles, the father of Theodosius – Emperor Theodosius, Athena, male and female figures.*
Inside the naos we can see a part of the original podium which originally upheld the statue of Emperor Hadrian, venerated as a deity.

42

12 - HOUSES ON THE SLOPE

From the opposite part of the *Temple of Hadrian* the interesting complex of the so-called «Houses on the slope» faces out onto *Kuretes Street*. The privileged location in the heart of the city on the declivity of Mount Bülbül and the architecturally-elegant and sumptuous imprint lead us to believe that the houses were inhabited by the most qualified and wealthy social class, and for this reason they are also known as «richmen's houses». Their particular position on the slopes of the mountain enabled each house to serve as a covered terrace for the one next to it. Most of these houses had three floors, and opened up around a columned or porticoed central peristyle, whose function was to illuminate the inside rooms. Very often the peristyle was ornamented with a fountain or provided with a well, and was usually paved in marble. The houses were heated by a sys-

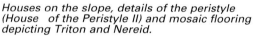

Houses on the slope, details of the peristyle (House of the Peristyle II) and mosaic flooring depicting Triton and Nereid.

Houses on the slope, details of the peristyle (House of the Peristyle I) and ruins of a fountain.

tem similar to the one used in spas. The inside rooms had frescoed walls depicting especially mythological subjects, while the floors were usually adorned with refined mosaics.

The event of their construction went back to the Augustan age, and there is reason to believe that they were used as residences at least until the 7th century: the date of the last evident reconstruction. In a later period, these houses were utilized as storehouses for cereals, and numerous water-mills were superimposed on them.

The so-called **House of the Peristyle II** was in fact distinguished by the presence of two courtyards and by the considerable profusion of decorations. Its dating is from the Ist century, even if it was rebuilt several times, at least until the 6th century. The main peristyle (B1) is the one which has reached us

Houses on the slope, details of interiors and frescoed walls.

in the best state of preservation. To be noted are the elegant columns which upheld the valuable Corinthian capitals. The flooring of the vestibule which runs inside the colonnade is formed of a two-toned mosaic which repeats geometric motifs. The floor mosaic depicting *the Triton and Nereid* in the south vestibule, exactly opposite a niche which opens in the wall, is particularly noteworthy. The niche is adorned with frescoes and mosaics (5th century), while the flooring is composed of two-tone marble mosaics. The ones depicting Dionysus and Ariadne surrounded by trees and animals stand out, while among the frescoes *Eros wearing a crown* excels. The numerous inside rooms have mosaic flooring and frescoes on the walls (4th century). The **House of the Peristyle I** has been restored, like the previously-mentioned one, to give visitors a chance to realize what the general arrangement of

Houses on the slope: two details of mosaic decorations and detail of the interior.

these Ephesian patrician residences had been. Originally, this had been a house with two floors occupying an area of 900 sq.m. Unfortunately, the complete collapse of the second floor made it impossible to rebuild even the slightest outline of it. Also in this house the peristyle (A2) represents the main architectonic element in a complex made up of twelve rooms, intended for the most diverse uses. The small but pretty courtyard is bordered by doric columns at its four corners; next to the marble paving on the north side stands out what remains of a fountain. The building of this residence goes back to the 1st century, as does the first mentioned one.

In the 5th century during works of rebuilding, a couple of rooms were added, placed to the rear of the fountain, which stood out because of their mosaic floorings and for the reddish tonalities of the frescoes. West of the peristyle, a room with elevated walls presented frescoes which have reached us in a good state of preservation.

The subjects of the paintings were inspired by theatrical motifs: it is for this reason that the room is known as «the theatre». Worthy of note are the motifs inspired by plays by Menandro and Euripides, while other frescoes represent male and female nudes. The fresco depicting the *Combat between Heracles and Acheloo* emerges due to its plastic values and high dramatic quality. The flooring of this room is covered with mosaic decorations datable, as the frescoes, to the 2nd century. Among other interesting rooms we recall the kitchen, and the bath which gives us the opportunity to appreciate fully the ingenious heating system for the different inside rooms.

49

13 - BATHS OF SCHOLASTICA

The main thermal complex in Ephesus was located above *Kuretes Street* behind the *Temple of Hadrian*. Its foundation was between the second half of the 1st century and the beginning of the 2nd century. It owes its name to Scholastica, a Christian woman who in 400 provided for the complete rebuilding of the complex, utilizing for the new construction stone and marble materials coming from other buildings and monuments in the city.

The prediliction which the Romans had for the thermal institution – widely spread to all corners of the Empire – is well known. Although it declined during the medieval period, the baths were newly evaluated in the Seljukian and Ottoman eras. Like all Roman baths, the Ephesian Baths of Scholastica followed the arrangement for the various rooms in accordance with the functions that took place in them. The *Apodyterium* was the room used as a dressing room; the *Sudatorium* corresponded to the modern sauna; the *Calidarium* was meant for ablutions and massages; the *Tepidarium* was reserved for not-

Houses on the slope, House of the Peristyle II.

Baths of Scholastica, headless statue of Scholastica and view of the ruins.

Calidarium of the Scholastica Baths.

very-hot baths, and was the room where people chatted and held forth on political and philosophical topics; the *Frigidarium* was the room intended for cold, stimulating baths.

It is believed that the original complex of the baths was set out on three floors: the vast area, strewn with ruins, is accessible from Kuretes Street, by means of a staircase located near the Temple of Hadrian, or from a cross-street located mid-way between the latter and the *Fountain of Trajan*. The dressing room must have been a very spacious room, with columns and niches. In one of these can still be seen – on a pedestal – the **headless statue of Scholastica**. The Frigidarium, annexed to the dressing room, contained an ellipitical swimming pool for cold water, at its centre. Through an ogival door

was the entrance to the Tepidarium, situated in the northern part of the dressing room. In this location was the entrance to the Calidarium, which is also the best preserved room. It is interesting to observe here – as in the other rooms – the rational and ingenious set-up of the water and air-heating system, fed by a hypocaust set up in the vicinity of the Calidarium.

The **Latrine** is annexed to the complex of the baths, and there are good reasons for believing that it was built in the early constructional phases of the said baths. The bathrooms and lavatories have come down to us in an excellent state of preservation: the floor is covered with mosaics, and the complex contributes to shedding light on the organization of the plumbing facilities in the ancient city.

This building, too, attributable by its ruins to a house with a peristyle, was part of the thermal complex and of the public toilets. Its construction is datable, therefore, to the Trajan period.

An inscription discovered in the latrine clarifies the function of this building. The brothel was originally on two floors, but today only the ruins of the first floor remain. It is supposed that the rooms of the upper floor were reserved for the girls, while those of the ground floor were assigned to receiving the customers. In the main area, a dining room has been discovered; the traces of several frescoes are poor and of little worth, while the mosaic-decorated flooring depicting the *Seasons* is significant (those representing *Autumn* and *Winter* are the best preserved).

In an adjoining bathroom, originally supplied with hot and cold water, are several remarkable mosaics which depict *Three Ladies Drinking*, *A Servant Standing*; *A Rat Busy Eating Crumbs of Food*, and *A Cat*. At the side of the building was a well inside of which has been discovered a curious and obscene terracotta *statue of Priapus*, on display at the *Ephesus Museum*.

Brothel, view of the ruins from Kuretes Street.

15 - LIBRARY OF CELSIUS

The very elegant perspective of this building, put back in its place after patient restoration work, does justice to the original splendour of this building which is numbered among the most relevant and most visited vestiges of Ephesus. The library was built during the Imperial Age, at the time of Hadrian, and was erected by Tiberius Julius Aquila who desired that it be dedicated to his father, Tiberius Julius Caesar Poleameanus: formerly Roman Consul and governor of the Asian province during the years around 105-107 A.D. The building was begun in 114, and was concluded in 135 by Tiberius J. Aquila's heirs, to whom a bequest of money was left so that they would provide for the purchase of books and for the maintenance of the complex.

In the second half of the 3rd century, at the time of the invasions by the Goths, the inside of the edifice was completely devastated by a fire which fortunately spared the external structures of the façade. Several restorations came about at the turn of the 4th century. From these times dates the construction of a fountain which long reflected the indicative outline of the perspective of the library. During excavation works, several enormous protruding marble blocks, which made up the edges of the fountain, were discovered. These blocks, transferred to the *Museum of Vienna*, were part of a commemorative monument erected in celebration of the victories of Marcus Aurelius and L. Vero over the Parthians. Around the 10th century, the façade was razed to the ground by a telluric motion.

The Library as it appears to us today reveals elements of distinguished architecture. The façade is

Library of Celsius, view of the complex with pedestal bearing an inscription.

Library of Celsius, façade and entrance stairway.

Library of Celsius, details of the façade (central part with friezes) and details of sculptures.

Following pages, two details of 1st and 2nd orders of columns of the Library of Celsius.

embellished with the scenic effect of two rows of columns. Those on the first floor, upholding Corinthian capitals, are arranged in four couples at the summit of the entrance staircase, made of nine steps. The columns of the upper floor are more reduced in dimensions compared to those on the lower floor. The columns of the three central pairs upheld architectural elements in the shape of triangular and semi-circular pediments. On the lower floor, behind the scenographic colonnade, three doors are framed by very valuable ornamental motifs, in the manner of friezes in relief and surmounted by the same number of windows. The central door is larger in dimensions than the side doors. Smaller windows open up also on the upper floor. On the first floor of the façade, several niches – carefully sunken between exquisitely worked jambs – hold four sculpted figurations. Inscriptions engraved on the pedestals inform us that the statues represent several of Celsius's qualities, namely *Virtue* (*sophia*) *Knowledge* (*episteme*), *Sagacity* (*arete*) and *Fortune* (*ennoia*). These sculptures are copies, as the originals were transferred to Vienna during archaeological-type displays.

On the vaulted wall of the Library, in a tomb underneath the niche, has been discovered the sarcophagus of Celsius, made of carved marble and decorated with reliefs representing *Eros and Nike*, and ornamental figurations such as garlands and rosettes. The presence of the sarcophagus calls to mind the primary origin of the site, conceived as a mausoleum in memory of Celsius.

The apse contained the statue of Celsius (or of his son), which at present can be seen in the *Archaeological Museum of Istanbul*. The original arrangement of the inside of the Library was supposedly divided into three floors; the inside sections of the masonry structures reveal the presence of rows of niches where once rolls of parchment and books were set out.

16 - MARBLE STREET

This street, which practically constitutes the entrance to the *theatre* for anyone coming from the *Library of Celsius*, goes along the western slopes of Mount *Panayır Dağı*, in a zone of considerable architectural interest. Its origins date from the 1st century A.D., but a rebuilding which took place in the 5th century is definite, when a certain *Eutropius* provided for its paving, using uneven marble blocks which won for it its name. This street served the carriage traffic: the deep grooves of the wheels are still visible in the parts that were subject to restoration during the High Medieval period. On the sides of the street are visible the ruins of a Roman columned portico and of a podium on which a covered stoa stood, built during the reign of Nero and used mostly for pedestrian traffic.

Marble Street, general view, ruins of the columned portico and of the stoa.

The imposing and scenographical building opened up on the western flanks of the mountain, directionally turned towards the plain strewn with antique ruins and travelled by the charming profile of *Arcadian Street*. The theatre has come down to us in a wonderful state of preservation, and constitutes one of the best-preserved buildings in the entire archaeological zone. It is one of the most amazing and attractive evidences of this type of architecture, which was very widespread throughout the entire Mediterranean basin.

Its first construction dates from the Hellenistic period, and was undertaken at the time of Lysimachus. Over the course of the centuries, various modifications were made which culminated in the substantial rebuilding that took place during the Roman era.

During the Imperial Age, under Claudius (41-54 A.D.) the building was enlarged and finished under Trajan (98-117 A.D.). To the age of Nero (54-68 A.D.) are datable the first two floors of the stage, which was finished (together with the rebuilding of the auditorium) under Settimus Severus (193-211 A.D.).

As with all similar constructions, the Ephesian theatre follows a division into three main sections: *Skene* (the proscenium), *Orchestra* (place for scenic action) and *Cavea* (space reserved for the audience). The primitive stage of the original Hellenistic building was formed by a low proscenium adorned with architectural elements. The one built in the Imperial Age was developed on three floors, and was enriched by columns upholding triangular or semicir-

Theatre, view from Arcadian Way.

Following pages, panorama from the summit of the Theatre with a view of the ruins and the Arcadian Way.

Views of the Theatre and ruins of the stage.

cular tympani, while a great profusion of sculptures was set up inside the niches. The auditorium, still used today for seating the public during the performances in the theatre, is arranged in three large semi-circles broken up by eleven wedges of steps separated by entrance staircases. The original theatre could seat about 24,000; the auditorium originally rose for at least 30 metres over the orchestra, and was crowned at the summit by a porticoed structure which had the function of further improving the acoustics in the complex. The theatrical productions in the classical period were performed by male actors who wore masks on their faces. These and other elements related to the social life in Ephesus during its period of greatest splendour have been inferred from the frescoes decorating several walls of the so-called *Houses on the slope*.

This street, laid out in the Hellenistic Age, was the main entrance road to the city for whoever was arriving from the *Port*. It was, therefore, known as Port Street. Between the end of the 4th century and the beginning of the 5th century, Arcadius – son of Theodosius, who reigned over the Eastern Roman Empire – began considerable rebuilding work. An epigraph informs us that the street called *Arcadian* from that time on was lighted at night by a sequence of 50 lamps, spaced out along the 500 metres of its length.

This was a very unusual fact in antiquity when one thinks that only cities like Rome and Antioch enjoyed the same privilege. We can therefore realize the importance which Ephesus still held at the dawning of the Middle Ages. The wide road (11 m) was flanked on the sides by columned porticos, the pavements of which had precious mosaic decorations.

These porticos, which were reserved for pedestrians, had the function of protecting them from the bad weather, and hosted shops in the inner part. The roadway, completely covered with marble, was enriched – towards the middle part – by four columns culminating in Corinthian capitals which upheld statues of the Four Evangelists.

The shafts of the columns, still in existence, denote ornamental patterns of clearly Christian imprint.

Arcadian Way, detail of a sculpture, view towards the Theatre and 6th-century column.

There is reason to believe that this latter decorative element is the result of an addition made under Justinian (6th century), shortly before the inexorable decline of the city.

19 - CHURCH OF THE MOST HOLY VIRGIN

The considerable ruins of this building rise at a short distance from the ancient *Port*, and this fact partially supports the hypothesis that originally it was a place for the exchange of grain commodities and money. Other hypotheses are in favour of the idea that it housed a finishing school for Ephesian priests. It is known for certain that its first construction took place, still in the Roman era, around the 2nd century and that it was subsequently transformed into a Christian basilica in the 4th century.

The original design of the building was with three naves: the changes brought about in the 4th century followed the outline of a Christian basilica, with the addition of a baptismal font in the northern part of the vestibule. The central nave, equally as wide as the apse, was flanked by narrower side naves divided from the central one by a colonnade and by other architectural elements.

The church is also famous as the *Church of the Council* since in 431 it entertained the Assizes that

In these pages, Church of the Most Holy Virgin with details of the ruins and remains of the colonnade.

had the task of confuting the Nestorian Heresy, sanctioning the divine nature of Christ and the dogma of the divine motherhood of Mary.

Certainly this building – further enlarged and provided with a cupola at the time of Justinian (6th c.) – is the first place of worship dedicated to the Virgin Mary; it was erected on the site of a house in which the Madonna lived during her stay in Ephesus.

The tradition that Mary, entrusted to St John by the crucified Christ, spent the remaining years of her life in Ephesus, then coming there to be buried, was sealed also by a pastoral visit which Pope Paul VI made to Ephesus in 1967.

Subsequent to the transformations operated by Justinian, a smaller basilica was erected next to the original building, which earned for the entire complex the title of *Double Church*.

Located to the east of the Acropolis, at the foot of *Panayır Dağı*, the Stadium, measuring 230 metres long and 30 metres wide, is shaped like a horse-shoe.

The Stadium had an important place in the lives of Ephesians since in antiquity, various sports competitions like boxing, and wrestling etc. were held there. The entrance of the Stadium is located in the west. The *gate* at the entrance, with its double row of columns, resembled a triumphal arch. The vase and the plaques, decorated with rabbit motifs, and visible in front of the entrance facing the street, were brought here from another location. The seats located at the foot of the hill were carved out of natural rock in the form of steps. The other side was raised with vaulted galleries and the seats were placed on them. These vaulted galleries resemble long rooms and every seven to eight metres there are small holes which open into the rooms.

The Stadium was built during the Hellenistic era, and was restored to its present condition during the reign of Nero (54-68). In the 3rd and the 4th centuries, the arched entrances to the west of the seats were altered.

During the 3rd and 4th centuries, gladiators and wild animal fights were very popular in the Roman world. These games were held in the stadiums and theatres in front of large audiences. Christians were murdered during these wild animal fights. This is why, after Christianity became the official religion, the Ephesus Stadium was destroyed unmercifully by religious fanatics, as though to take revenge.

Therefore today, there is not even one well-preserved row of seats to be found in the Stadium. Some of the exquisitely-crafted rows of seats with inscriptions on them were used in the construction and restoration of other buildings during the 4th and the 6th centuries.

Ephesus Stadium, traditional Camel fight.

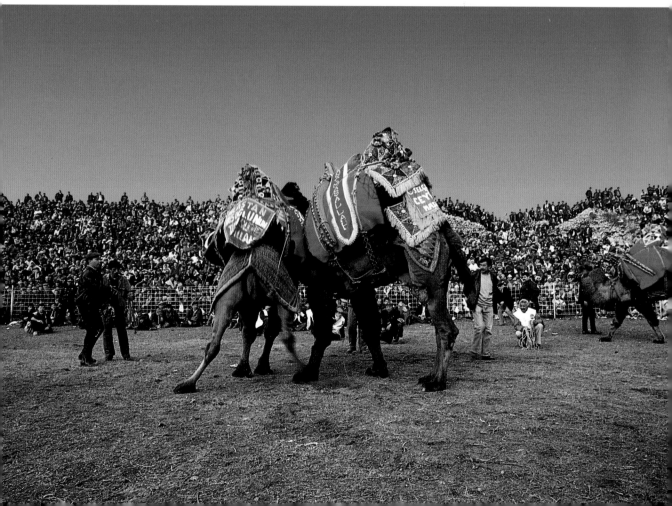

THE CAVE OF THE SEVEN SLEEPERS

The asphalt road that turns east by the *Vedius Gymnasium* leads to the Cave of the Seven Sleepers. The Christians in the early empire were in dispute with the Roman state over the subject of the imperial cult, according to which those Christians who refused to sacrifice animals at an imperial temple were considered enemies of the state, and were treated as such. The story of the Seven Sleepers is based on this dispute.

Around 250, during the reign of Emperor Decius, seven young Christian men escaped from the city and took refuge in a cave, since they had refused to sacrifice animals at the imperial temple. After a while these seven young men fell asleep, and when they woke up they went to the city to buy food. To their amazement, they found out that they had slept not for one night but for two hundred years, and that Christianity had spread to every corner of the Roman Empire. When Emperor Theodosius II heard of the incident, he accepted it as evidence of resurrection which was being discussed in the churches then. When these young men died, following an impressive funeral they were buried in the cave where a church was later built. The excavations carried on here during 1927-1928 brought to light a *church* and several hundred *graves* which dated to the 5th and 6th centuries. *Inscriptions* dedicated to the Seven Sleepers were found on the walls of the church and in the graves.

For hundreds of years, people wanted to be buried as close as possible to the Seven Sleepers, who were considered holy. According to a Christian belief, St Mary Magdalene is also buried here.

Two images of the Cave of the Seven Sleepers.

According to St John's Gospel, before His death. Jesus pointed at St John and said, «Woman, here is your son» and then pointed at the Virgin Mary and said «Here is your mother». The minutes of the Ecumenical Council of 431 indicate that four or six years after the death of Jesus. St John and the Virgin Mary came to Ephesus together, and for a short time stayed in the building, a section of which is now under the Church of the Virgin Mary. Later, St John moved the Virgin Mary to a house that he had prepared for her on Bülbül Daği. As time went by, the location of the house where Mary spent the last days of her life was forgotten, and it fell into ruins. Yet, shortly after the Middle Ages, the location of the house was often discussed again, but no conclusion could be reached.

In 1878, Clément Brentano published the relevations of a German nun named Catherine Emmerich in *The Life of the Virgin Mary* written in French. The work brought new interest to the subject of the location of the Virgin Mary's house. In 1891, Eugene Poulin, a Lazarist priest who was the presi-

House of Mary, general view and detail of the interior.

House of Mary, interior.

dent of Izmir College, in order to check the validity of his devoted nun's revelations, entrusted a group under the leadership of a priest named Yung, with the search for the house. The group searched for a long time on the mountains south of Ephesus, and finally found the house on Panayır Dağı, known as the House of the Virgin Mary.

Catherine Emmerich (1774-1824) had never left the town where she was born, yet her description of the house of Mary exactly fits the house at *Panaya Kapulu*. In order to introduce the house to the world, Eugène Poulin published a series of articles and succeeded in attracting a lot of attention. Most of the religious experts who visited the house accepted it as the house of the Virgin Mary. The patriarch of Izmir, Monseigneur Timoni, after serious research, gave permission in 1892 to conduct religious ceremonies there. In 1961, Pope John XXIII put an end to the dispute that was still going on over the location of the house of the Virgin Mary, by announcing it to be a place of pilgrimage. In 1967, Pope Paul VI and, in 1979, Pope John Paul II visited the house, thus indicating the importance that they placed on the house.

The road which stretches from the Magnesia Gate toward Bülbül Dağı reaches the house. The remains of a *round cistern* in the small square located 100 metres from the house, and its arched wall on the side facing the hill, were discovered first. The steps on the side of the cistern are completely destroyed; only a section which resembles a pool is extant. During the course of excavations carried on near the wall, two *sarcophagi* made of baked clay were discovered. Each contained a skeleton, the skulls of which were turned toward the house, and burial gifts. One of the two coins found in the sarcophagi belonged to the reign of Emperor Constantine and the other to the reign of Emperor Justinian.

House of Mary, general view.

The Statue of the Virgin Mary.

There is a small domed church with a cross-shaped plan at the end of the road that leads from the cistern. This building is known as the *House of the Virgin Mary* and dates to the 6th-7th centuries.

When it was discovered, only its foundation and parts of its walls were standing. It has been restored to its present state. In order to indicate the original walls, a red line was drawn between these and the new walls. An entrance with door-like niches on both sides, leads into a vaulted vestibule whence one enters the hall with an apse. The **statue of the Virgin Mary** found in the apse had been placed there about one hundred years ago. Since the grey area in front of the apse is different from the rest of the marble-paved floor, it must have been the location of the hearth. The pieces of coal found during excavations and a section of the foundation have

been dated to the first century. The small room in the south is known as the bedroom; there is an apsidal niche in its eastern wall. Since the Virgin Mary is also revered by Muslims, they pray (perform namaz) in this room. Inscriptions seen on the walls are interpretations of the section of the Koran relating to the Virgin Mary. Also, for those who want further information, there are many Korans in different languages in a special chest. The remains of another room which should be located symmetrically to this one have not been discovered yet. On the second terrace to the west of the house, there are fountains, the waters of which supposedly have medicinal qualities.

The water supply for these fountains comes from under the pink-coloured marble floor covering in the bedroom.

THE EPHESUS MUSEUM

Its first arrangement goes back to 1929. Its reconstruction was effected in 1964, while the most recent rebuilding (1976) has restored the present layout divided into seven rooms containing findings from the Artemision, the Basilica of St John and, in general, from the entire complex of archaeological excavations.

The reconstruction of the tympanun of the *Temple of Augustus* (or *of Isis*), is set out in the *Gardens of the Museum* with a display of the sculptures which used to decorate the frieze, then located near the *Fountain of Pollione*. The marble sundial with epigraph is from the 3rd century A.D. In this setting are also located interesting sarcophagi of various periods.

The Room of *Findings from Houses* holds materials come to light during excavations in Ephesian residences. For the most part, these are small statues, furnishings, busts, frescoes and fragments of mosaic. Remarkable are the frescoes depicting the *philosopher Socrates* (2nd c.); the sculpture depicting *Artemis the Huntress*, a Roman work of the 2nd century; the small bronze reproducing *Eros astride the Dolphin* (2nd c.); and, among the mosaics, the *Head of Medusa* and the *Head of Dionysus*, Roman works of the 5th century.

Ephesus Museum, the gardens, detail of the tympanum of the Temple of Augustus.

Ephesus Museum, details of the friezes in Hadrian's Temple.

Eros on a Dolphin.

A floor mosaic, a house foundling.

Eros with a Rabbit.

An Egyptian Priest.

Head of Socrates.

The *Room of Findings from Fountains* is almost entirely dedicated to the sculptural fittings and ornamentations which decorated the city's fountains. Among the outstanding elements in this room we can recall several sculptures discovered near the *Fountain of Pollione*, namely: the marble depicting the *Warrior's Rest* (2nd c.); the *Head of Zeus*, and the mutilated *Statue of Aphrodite*. both of the 1st c. A.D.; the *Group of Polyphemus* (1st c. A.D.), formerly an ornament on the pediment of the *Temple of Augustus*. From the *Fountain of Trajan* came the partly-mutilated marble *Dionysus*, the Roman copy of an original Greek marble of the 5th c. B.C.; the mutilated marble depicting *Androcles* (2nd c.); and a coeval semi-nude and mutilated figuration of *Aphrodite*. An interesting sculpture – even if lacking in its fundamental parts – reproduces a *Nymph* com-

ing from the *Fountain of Laecanius Bassus*. The bearded head of a Military Commander crowned with a helmet is from the 2nd c. A.D., and was discovered along *Marble Street*.

The so-called *Room of Findings of Recent Date* preserves evidences from the Byzantine period, fragments of a 10th-century icon, uncovered silver panels, stone medals with paintings, documentation of numismatic interest, a glass tray from the 1st c. A.D., terracotta wine jugs (6th-2nd c. B.C.). To be noted are the findings brought to light in the theatre, such as masks and objects of everyday use such as oil-lamps (4th c. B.C.-6th c. A.D.). Outstanding are an ivory-like frieze, discovered in one of the «Houses on the slope» and depicting – on three panels – *Episodes of Trajan's war against the Barbarians* (2nd c. A.D.), and a coeval marble bust representing *Emperor Marcus Aurelius*.

General view of the Room of Findings from Fountains.

Marble sculpture depicting the Warrior's Rest.

Ephesus Museum, details of sculptures
(a nymph, Androcles, Dionysus, Aphrodite).

In the *Room of Funeral Findings* are set out the contents of tombs discovered during archaeological excavations. The oldest tomb discovered in the Ephesian territory goes back to the Mycaenean period: inside it were found objects datable from the 15th-14th c. B.C. A funeral stele depicting a *Married couple with their children* goes back to the 2nd c. A.D. Among the various sarcophagi stands out the one referred to as *Klozomena* (from the name of an ancient city located west of Smirna), containing the objects accompanying a dead man and datable from the 5th c. B.C. Also remarkable are Phoenician glasses, Byzantine bracelets and a sculptural figuration of Cybele (6th c. B.C.).

In the *Room of the Ephesian Artemis* are kept the

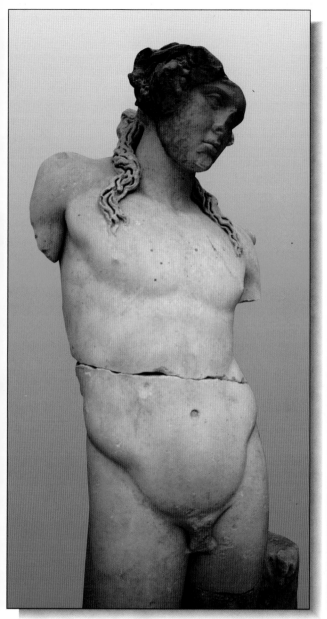

most illustrious representations of the goddess and the findings brought to light in the *Artemision* and near the *Altar of Artemis*. The so-called *Great Artemis* is a marble of the 1st c. A.D., upholding two lions on her shoulders and bearing a large quantity of sculptural ornaments. The forearms are missing at the height of the peculiar band that girds her abdomen, recalling a symbolism connected with fertility. The other statue of the goddess is known as the *Beautiful Artemis* (2nd c. A.D.). It slightly antedates the former, but it has been sculpted in most precious marble, originally gilded. On the sides she is flanked by sacred hinds; this, too, recalls the theme of fertility already present in the first one. Among the other figurations of Artemis we can recall a headless

sculpture of the 2nd century A.D. and a *Back of the Goddess* (1st c. B.C.). Among the numerous findings in the Artemision stand out several gold statuettes of the 7th century B.C. and ivory sculptures from the same period. In the *Room of Portraits and Imperial Cults* are arranged interesting portraits; we can recall different representations of *Augustus* (1st c. A.D.), a *Head of Trajan* (1st-2nd c. A.D.), a *Portrait of Germanicus* (1st c. A.D.), a *Head of Nero* (1st c. A.D.), and a *Head of Commodus* (2nd c.A.D.). Over all, however, stand out the delightful sculptured figurations which used to decorate the friezes of the *Temple of Hadrian* (2nd c. A.D.) and which were removed from their original location in order to preserve them from bad weather.

Ephesus Museum, sculptures depicting Marcus Aurelius, Zeus, and a military leader.

The Polyphemus Group.

Frieze describing the East Campaign of Emperor Trajan. Ivory.

A view of the Ephesus Museum courtyard.

The sundial.

«Beautiful Artemis» flanked by sacred hinds.

The Great Artemis, marble, 1st-century. AD.

Relics from the Artemision.

Part of a statue of Artemis.

*Head and arm of Emperor
Domitian, 81-96 A.D.*

*Bust of a man, marble, 3rd-
century A.D.*

*Head of man, marble 2nd-
century A.D.*

Statue of Consul Stefanos.

THE VILLAGE OF ŞIRINCE

Situated on the northern slope of a mountain, the village of Şirince is 8 km. to the east of the province of Selçuk. Until 1920, Şirince was the center for trade in the region. It is said that the natives of Şirince are the descendents of the last residents of Ephesus. The train station in the province di Selçuk, which used to be called Ayasuluk, connects the village to the other cities in the vicinity. According to the exchange policy set by the rules of the peace treaty at the end of World War I, the natives of the village were moved to Greece and some of the Turks there were brought and settled here. Şirince is famous for its *drinking water*, *gardens* and especially its *wines*. Its *18th and 19th century houses*, which are still in use, are extremely interesting. These wooden houses bear the characteristics of the Mediterranean architecture peculiar to the region. They line the narrow streets with sidewalks. Some houses have bay windows, and most of them have wide façades with many windows.

Frescoes decorate the areas around the windows and under the bay windows of certain houses. The interiors of these two-storey houses are decorated with frescoes and woodwork. There are two old churches on the flat land at the western end of the village. The walls and the portico are built in a style popular in the area. The rectangular panels on thick layers of plaster are decorated with frescoes depicting saints. The church, which is assumed to have been built in the 19th century, is in very poor condition. The other church is known both as «the church with a dome» and «the stone church». Its dome and vaults are supported by columns. The church is being repaired by the Ephesus Museum. The inscription seen on the entrance was placed there during this renovation.

The inscription states: «The Church of Johannes, the well known prophet of God, and the godfather, was built from its foundation, under the supervision of the dear bishop of sacred Heliapolis of one of the rulers of Kallinicos of Uifne. A lot of money was collected to complete the construction of the church. When the completed structure was destroyed, with the help of God and Johannes, the baptizer. The church was rebuilt, and the structure was completed in September of 1805». According to the inscription, the church was built for John (Johannes), the Baptist.

The Şirince Village is a place where traditional Anadolu life survives. It is supposed that the Virgin Mary is buried here.

KUŞADASI

The importance of this town, located in a picturesque site overlooking the gulf of the same name stretching out towards the Aegean, depends as much on its atmosphere and landscape as it does on the fact that it is an ideal point of departure for excursions. Kuşadası is in fact a charming seaside resort with good hotels and restaurants, as well as functional, well-equipped international tourist complexes. The surroundings furnish the occasion to admire some of the most qualified and interesting archaeological sites in all of Turkey: from Ephesus to Priene, Miletus, Colophon. The spacious gulf of Kuşadası is circumscribed on the north by an irregular peninsular appendix which separates it from the gulf of Izmir, terminating opposite the island of Chios. In the southern portion a promontory extends towards the island of Samos, leaving a narrow arm

of the sea open. In front of the inhabited center, on an isle connected by a road to the mainland, rises the **Kücükada Kalesi**, an ancient fortress still surrounded by imposing turreted glacis. This fortress became famous during the 16th century when it was used as a base for the exploits of the pirate Khair ad-Din, better known as *Barbarossa*.

Together with his brothers, the famous corsair raged along the Aegean coasts of North Africa, and established a small kingdom in Algeria which served as a bridgehead for further conquests in the Mediterranean basin. After the occupation of Tunis (1533), the Turkish sultan Süleyman entrusted him with the command of the Ottoman fleet against Charles V and the marine republics of Venice and Genoa, which he long kept at bay, acquiring great prestige and riches.

A view of the Kuşadası Marina.

Scenery from the Kadınlar Hamamı district, Kuşadası.

The picturesque port of Kuşadası.

INDEX

EPHESUS
Project and editorial conception: Casa Editrice Bonechi
Graphic design and Make-up: Manuela Ranfagni. *Editing:* Anna Baldini
Translated by Carolyna Cotchett, Studio Comunicare, Florence

ISBN 88- 8029-591-8

* * *